Mournes in Motion

A Collection of Poetry and Prose from Newcastle Writers' Group

Copyright © NEWCASTLE WRITERS' GROUP 2023
ISBN: 9798387298486

All rights reserved. No part of this publication may be reproduced, stored in a retrieval system, or transmitted in any form or by any means (electronic, mechanical, photocopying, scanning, recording or otherwise) without the prior written permission of the copyright owner of this book. Any person who does any unauthorized act in relation to this publication may be liable to criminal prosecution and civil claims for damages.

The members of the Newcastle Writers' Group have been asserted under the Copyright, Designs and Patents Act 1988 UK to be the authors of this work.

First Edition 2023

This book is sold subject to the condition that it shall not, by way of trade or otherwise, be lent, re-sold, hired out, or otherwise circulated without the author's prior consent in any form of binding or cover other than that in which it is published.

This novel is a work of fiction. Any references to historical events, real people, or real locales are used fictitiously. Other names, characters, places and incidents are the product of the author's imagination and any resemblance to actual events, locales, or persons living or dead is entirely coincidental.

Available as a Kindle eBook and paperback from Amazon.com, Amazon.co.uk and Amazon's other retail outlets and websites.

Learn more about the Newcastle Writers' Group on our website: www.newcastlewritersgroup.com

CONTENTS

SPRING 5

    The Glen River 7

    In My Head 9

    Bryansford Blackbird 10

    Radiance 11

    The Coney Island Whelks Picking Man 12

    Tollymore Running 14

    Solace 16

    Mourne Wall Challenged 17

    For Friends 26

SUMMER 27

    Amelia and Me 29

    The Meaning of Life 31

    Newcastle Harbour To Millstone 32

    1911 Census 34

    The Newcastle Snake 36

    Father's Day 38

    Foggy windows 40

    Moon Beam Room 42

AUTHUMN 45

    Rathfriland Red Kites 47

    Ploughing Fields 48

    Shadowland 50

    An Uncertain Welcome 51

    Night Duty 52

    In Donard Forest 53

    Missing You is my Mourne Mountain View 54

    The Newcastle Harbour Swimmers 56

    The Waterfall 58

WINTER 63

    Newcastle Fishing Disaster 65

    Lakeside View (Castlewellan Forest Park) 68

    Spirit of Wind and Rain 70

    The Mark 72

    Harbour Lights 80

    A Snowy Night in Mourne 82

    Cold Winter's View 84

    A Winter's Walk up Donard 86

    Dundrum Speakeasy 88

Biographies 89

SPRING

THE GLEN RIVER

Harry Mitchell

On the mountain top, precipitation won't stop,
Causing tributaries to mingle and merge.
A creation of weather, they're stronger together,
As they begin to swell and then surge.

Gravity's winning, they're tumbling they're spinning.
They're out of control as they strive for their goal.
Bumping and barging now everyone's charging,
When will the excitement end!

Violently swaying, off rocks ricocheting,
With particles racing and boulders displacing,
It's all so thrilling, they're bursting they're spilling.
Nothing can stand in their way!

With everything churning, there's no time for turning,
But then they take flight----and a temporary respite,
As they land in a pool of foam.
Slowly gathering pace, it's not over this race,

And no time for calling this home.
It's onward they travel, more stones now, more gravel.
Released from the trees and embraced by the breeze,
It's wilder more free as they race to the sea.

Again, tumbling and turning and rushing and gushing,
Bumping and barging with everyone charging.
I've nothing but praise, as they welcome the waves,
Then together as one, they continue their fun,

And return to the foam, that they now call their home.
It's natures delight, to have witnessed this sight,
From where they have come,
To where they have gone.

IN MY HEAD

Elizabeth McCann

I write poems in my head
As I walk
On the bus
At night in bed

The words
Sparkle
Mesh
And dance gently together
Nudging close in harmony

Then
When I try to write them down
They darken
Become stubborn
Push away in sullenness
They don't want to be tied to the page
They want to dance in my head

BRYANSFORD BLACKBIRD

Liz Laird

Each morning, my blackbird opens his song,
in the wild rose by our bedroom, highest branch strong.
To his wakeful warbling, my spirit grows still,
Peace, blessed Peace, while the Mournes lie asleep.

His head raises up now, flute open, clear.
Notes drifting freely, float easy on breeze.
Opening the window, fresh air intertwines
filtering, fluttering, lilting music inside.
I gaze on my Love, through him, we are buoyed,
and bathing in melody; in unbridled joy!

Each day receives all in a new starting point,
And the risen sun promises heating up from the chill.
Open the self, hark, listen, birdsong,
proclaiming in blessings, that all do belong.

RADIANCE

Peter McCarron

January-sea calms the river.
The Sun-rise radiates glory.
Overpowering, imbibing senses full.
Rapturing the Earth's love-story.

You'd think it was human-made
That fluffy golden ring of old.
Mountains of Mourne awakening, to
Light on Earth, magic to behold.

Dependency of Earth-life, awaits,
The Sun to be seen.
Morning starts and evening ends
Of the day just been.

Humans can radiate light.
So too, Animals, plants and flowers
Bring light into humans' lives
Sun radiates life-giving powers.

THE CONEY ISLAND WHELKS PICKING MAN

Siobhan McElroy

I met him picking whelks on the strand,
this Coney Island fragile fingered man.
Conveyed to me the knowledge of his skill,
colour, shape and size, the ones that make you ill.
If in doubt, Throw it out!
Buckets yellow to the brim,
three bags full, tide brought in!
Lots of money to be made, in this periwinkle trade!
Oyster beds, at the bottom of the sea,
"Nothing left to cover me!"
On I walked with my furry friend
the length of the beach and back again.
In my heart I felt an ache - Emotions did Awake!
Hunger pains with bodies thin,
along this coast they must have been,
driven by famine and despair,
my native souls that perished there!
With bony hands did they hold them tight,
thankful for the tides delight?
If in doubt Throw Them Out!

I met him picking whelks on the strand,

this Coney Island whelks picking man.

Conveyed to me the knowledge of his skill,

colour, shape and size, the ones that make you ill!

The sun was low, I waved goodbye

The sea birds sang,

Now a distant shadow on the strand

This Coney Island Whelks picking man

This Coney Island Whelicks picking man!

TOLLYMORE RUNNING

Liz Laird

Running through Tollymore Forest – Go Breath Flow.
Winter retreating, Spring softening, under tow.
Over the monument, glimpses of the sun, so low,
washing in on the sea, in a warming glow.

A squirrel bounces out, red, dashes up and away.
A breeze circles in, trees gather, mumble and sway.
More surefooted now, I speed up on the lay,
dissecting the Arboretum's green, silvers and grey.

Running faster and freer, I release from life's fight,
then down on the gravel path, my soul takes to flight,
my torso, an air machine, my limbs, feather light.
All too soon, basking in sun glades, the hut is in sight.

The bushes are bristling, as I close in on Horn Bridge,
birds, chirping earlier in dawn choir, still laying siege.
The first people arriving now, remain out of reach,
but at one with the oak, strawberry tree, and the beech.

Thoughts gathered; I greet others. Silent waves respect space.
Up towards the Gothic Arch, runs in a slow pushing pace.
Time and truth do not rush; it's my prayer, not a race.
I leave my breath, and my foot fall, no other trace.

SOLACE

Elizabeth McCann

It's May
The air smells of pine
My fingers are sticky with sap
It's quiet here among the trees
I hear the water over the rocks
Tumbling
Splashing

Take all the
What ifs
Could have
Should have
Carry them away
There is only now
Move on

MOURNE WALL CHALLENGED

Lee Harding

The Mourne Wall Challenge follows a twenty-one mile trail along the delightful slopes of South Down's most famous mountain range. This story recounts my first attempt, an act of hubris which resulted in — as performances fuelled by pride often are — miserable failure.

I set off from Donard car park with dreams of glory on a grey day. The guidebooks stressed to start from the opposite end of the track but I was made of sterner stuff. After all, what was an extra two or three miles to a mighty man of the Mournes?

The rain struck mid-way up as I met the wall at the Saddle and didn't cease until I hit Binnian several hours later. I passed a couple taking a stroll at the highest peak which on the surface might not seem odd. The fact that it was six o'clock in the morning and that they had no rucksack, water or food raised my suspicions. They wore what amounted to a bathing suit and slippy trainers as the downpour drowned us all. That told a tale I had no desire to hear. I shook my head at how obtuse tourists could be and continued to the next leg of my journey.

One thing you must understand is my propensity to prepare. Every stretch of the trek was carefully mapped out with a printed hardcopy in my pack as a spare. Yet, when I reached to the summit of Slieve Binnian, I wondered which way to go. The Mourne Wall traces the countryside for miles, weaving like an undulating snake. 'Simply follow the wall and you can't go wrong,' they say, and I, like a fool, believed them. As in all instructions, the devil is in the detail. I soon discovered that the Wall splits incessantly and taking the wrong path can set you back several hours. Like an *eejit*, as the local parlance would affirm, I chose poorly. When I realised my mistake, my ego pushed out its chest and soldiered on regardless. The destination was the Silent Valley, a tourist beauty spot nestled within a lowland basin that lead to the perils of Slieve Muck.

I could see my error unfold to the south as I marched down a steep slope heading west. The mouth of the reservoir swallowed its prize through a giant plughole that siphoned the water into the bottom basin. That was the next flag on my map, but my current trajectory pointed to a spot a mile further on. I had half a mind to cut across and rejoin the main trail but the way was choked by a thicket of brambles which weren't congenial to my bare, hairy legs. So downwards I went, hugging tight to the shadow of the wall, reducing my speed as the descent took a deep dive.

One factor I failed to consider was what lay at the bottom. I could see the tarmac path that paralleled the reservoir shore but blocking the way was a rusty barbedwire fence. Before that treacherous obstacle lay a forest of gorse with spikes aplenty ready to rip into my flesh. I looked back up the mountain with a half-hearted hope. Thorns be damned, I said. I would push through them, jump over the fence, march to the mouth and rejoin my quest.

The barge through the briers made me hiss through my teeth. My legs are made of sterner stuff, I told myself as the jags bit in like a brood of rats. Each step drew a little blood which I wiped away with sweaty palms. The saving grace was the sun that now split the skies and bathed my destination in sparkling blues. I was now mere metres away from the fence. I focused on the barbs, looking for a fractured spot that I could climb over without the need of a tetanus injection. That was my fatal flaw.

The crack in the rock was hidden by a bastard bramble. My boot found its footing but when my weight went down so did I. My ankle twisted to the left as I plummeted right headlong into the loving embrace of a thousand thorns. I barely managed to push out my hands and caught myself in a press-up position. I twisted my body around and made sure to sit with my leg out straight. My breath whistled through my teeth as I fought the urge to panic. I had planned for situations like these but when they happen miles from civilisation the isolation only serves to heighten the alarm.

One unwelcome feat was to remove my boot before the swelling made it impossible. I picked the thorns from my fingers then untied my bootlace. With an ever-so-gentle pull, I eased my throbbing foot from its shield and winced as the cool air struck. There were no obvious signs of damage, thank God. With a gentle prod, I diagnosed myself with a twisted ankle.

Although the Mournes attracts hikers to test their endurance it does not permit their modern technology. My phone had no signal so low to the valley. I flexed my foot and noticed there was some movement. That spurred me on. By the mouth of the reservoir was a visitor café. I could hobble down, ring for a taxi, and be home by noon. That was option A and appeared to be the most appealing and certainly the most sensible.

By now, you have probably grasped that 'sensible' and hiking for over twenty miles along a dangerous landscape don't go hand-in-hand. And so I pondered option B. I turned my neck to follow the reservoir to the dam at the top of the hill. Beyond that lay the second stretch of water and further along lay the Saddle and my descent back to the car. I estimated the mileage then multiplied the normal hiking time by a factor of two. It seemed reasonable to assume that I would be back for early evening.

Pride and stubbornness are twins separated at birth. At times they converge to take the charge which can lead to disaster or redemption. Perhaps it was my ego pushing out its chest again but I chose to go for glory. I had woken that morning in search of adventure and dam be damned, I was going to find it!

With a ginger touch, I slipped a support onto my foot and a fresh pair of socks and slid it back into its boot. The lace was tied tight to reduce the blood flow and I pushed myself to a crouching position. This was the moment of truth. Regardless of my insane intentions, I knew that if my body could no longer support my weight then any attempts of a hero's journey would be short lived. I grimaced as the ache struck like a metal pipe to the base of my leg but it held firm. I took a step of faith and was rewarded with a duller pang. Hoisting my pack over my shoulder, I tread with extra care and aimed for the rusty barbedwire fence.

I spotted a small gap a little further on. Brushing aside the bushes and their unforgiving spikes, I lifted my leg high and set it over the chain-links, careful not to snag anything that dangled, and dropped to the path below. The reservoir shone like a crystal and drew my attention from the buzzing in my head. This was the allure of the Mourne Mountains: the raw unfettered charm that you could experience only if you were willing to fight to see it. And fight I did. I turned north and started my ascent, following the gradual incline for the next few miles. I took my time at the beginning. My muscles had cooled; one silly sprint and something might tear. There could be no further mishaps. I might have been a fool but I was not stupid.

The towering dam appeared to have a leak as I approached. Gushing from its stomach came a surge of pressured water from the reservoir above. It cascaded into the narrow channel and flowed towards the Irish Sea. I mounted a steep set of steps and took one at a time to the peak. As I said, I don't like to look back, but I took a minute to relive my morning. The Mourne Wall Challenge was officially over, much to my chagrin: now, a new adventure awaited.

I had trekked this route only once as a teen. My friends and I had followed this inlet coast as it weaved around the shale slopes and sandy shores. Youthful exertion abandoned me just as my hopes of completing my course and so I limped over the jagged boulders towards my goal swimming in the fog in the distance. When I drew closer, I recalibrated my projected finishing time. The journey was taking longer than I had anticipated. Not only that but the mist had morphed into drizzle to dampen my spirits.

I stumbled onwards until I reached a natural fork in the river. To the west lay Hare's Gap and to the east the Saddle and the car park. However, the way was blocked by a canyon with a roaring river running through its gulley. The other way was an open valley with an effortless slope. I knew I could walk from the Gap along a flat trail but it would add an extra hour of torture.

Guess which path I decided to take?

Wiping the sweat and spray from my brow, I set my resolve on the canyon. The water hastening by made me quicken my pace. I saw a waterfall further ahead and the breath in my body exhaled with a groan. I believe that most obstacles in life can be surmounted through wisdom, hard work, and determination. Setting your mind to a goal is not only altruistic but helps to drive the soul. Yet, some hurdles cannot be overcome.

The falls stretched the width of the canyon. A metric tonne of water dropped from its jaws and washed away my hope. I had no choice but to return to the crossroads and take the easier course.

I am not a fan of single choices so I craned my neck and stared up at the sky. The slopes that funnelled the canyon stretched to the horizon in a V but the incline was less than 40 degrees. If I could dig my good boot in and grip onto the purple heather I could pull myself up.

With another insane notion guiding my way, I jumped onto the green embankment. I had to scramble to keep still as gravity fought me tooth and claw. Gravel and dirt dug into my fingernails while the spectre of a sudden descent called me from below. I am not a fan of heights but ignored my frozen heart and battled upwards until, with one hand latched over the edge, I pulled myself to freedom.

By this time, I had hiked for nearly nine hours. The rumblings in my belly could no longer go unheeded so I sat on a rock and satisfied myself with a corned beef sandwich. I thought the higher vantage point would let me see the Saddle more clearly but that was when I realised my error. Not only was my destination not visible in the fog but it was the wrong stretch of mountain range. I had underestimated the distance by a considerable margin and with a quick recalculation deduced that the journey would take an additional three hours.

It is at these points that I take stock of my life. Why in the world was I up a mountain in the drizzling rain with an injured ankle and miles from home? You've probably been wondering the same thing. Surely, the challenge wasn't the only ingredient to this demented stew? That is true. There are other reasons why I was there, reasons that I do not wish to comment upon except to say that a transcendent task is a vital part of my core. Many men feel the same way. They need a goal to aspire to that tests the endurance of their soul. Only then is life worth living.

I took a long swig of water, pushed it into my pack, and set off. This was open hillside, less of an ascent but much harder to navigate without dropping into a ditch. Some sheep stopped chewing to watch the mad man walk by. I gave them a wave but they didn't respond in kind. They soon vanished as I rounded the bend and was confronted with my next impediment.

The river divided the landscape in two. Naturally, my journey took me to the other side. I slid down in a zigzag until I was level with the chopping froth. The rain had expedited the flow and I watched as a loose leaf barrelled its way by. There were a few solid looking rocks that I might use to cross but all were soaked. I recalled a time in winter when my friends and I tried to pass over an icy stretch. They went first with their longer legs while I lingered. A promise of a firm hand to catch geed me on and I launched myself to the bank. My so-called friend pulled away at the last second sending me to plummet into the icy depths. A thousand knives piercing your body is the perfect analogy. When I managed to clamber out, I had two minutes to remove my clothes before they froze and me in them.

This was the end of spring and although the river was bursting it would not rupture me. I used my right foot for support and stretched out with its injured twin. My toes tapped a rock in the centre and with a leap of faith, I leapt. I skipped from one spot to the next, praying that each would take my weight without slipping. I made it to the other side and immediately started to climb. Enough was enough: it was time to end the insanity.

I dragged myself to the path above and took a look around. The skies had split and the rain lashed down in torrents. My leg was cramping as I hobbled ever onwards. I scooped some water from a nearby stream and splashed my face clean. That revitalised my spirits and I staggered with greater strides. Not soon enough, I made it to a staircase made of rocks. I took them two at a time, fully ignoring the screaming from my lower half, and my heart leapt within me. There, less than a mile away, was Slieve Donard with the Saddle in its shadow.

I could almost touch my goal. The thought distracted from the blisters on my toes. I almost cried when my hands gripped the gravel as I hoisted myself onto the final trail. I unzipped my bag and hunted for a well-deserved treat. The last bite of granola bar disappeared just as I reached the Wall and I slumped against it with a smile. Twelve hours and God-knows how many miles had passed in self-inflicted pain but I had made it. It was the round trip from hell but my goal was accomplished for the day.

Except that I had yet to clamber over the style, descend the Dark Steps, cross the Glen River and trek for an hour to the car. But that is a story for another day.

FOR FRIENDS

Elizabeth McCann

Between us
We have made
A lattice
Fragile maybe
But mostly
Holding

A lattice of
Concern
Small kindnesses
Remembrances

A lattice of
Friendships and love
Holding us

SUMMER

AMELIA AND ME

Siobhan McElroy

Amelia and Me
walking on the promenade by the Irish Sea,
We're as happy as can be,
Amelia and me!

On the day that she was born, I whispered sweetly,
"I will love you always, you mean the world to me!"
And when she called me Daddy, my heart skipped with delight,
the riches of this world, I have within my sight!
On my shoulders high is where she likes to be,
smiling eyes, dimpled cheeks, singing merrily!

Amelia and Me
walking on the promenade by the Irish sea,
We're as happy as can be,
Amelia and me!

The stories that she tells of her dogs and cat

playing in the garden, Kitty scratching on the mat!

Love higher than the mountains deeper than the sea,

wider than the universe that's what she means to me!

Special times together stored within my heart,

The love I have for her grows when we're apart!

Amelia and Me

walking on the promenade by the Irish Sea,

We're as happy as can be,

Amelia and Me on the Promenade by the Irish Sea!

THE MEANING OF LIFE

Liz Laird

I woke early in June, a day ahead of myself.
I caught on quick, and mused gently,
on where I was in time and space,
and what is now.

The meaning of life
is the joy of each breath.
The foot strokes the earth
in each freedom felt step.
The birds chirp their way
in each leaf and branch sway.

There is nothing but this
in the tender love kiss
of Donard runner and world
twist inner, outer air swirls.

NEWCASTLE HARBOUR TO MILLSTONE

Harry Mitchell

We left the harbour without a care,
And crossed the road to the granite stair.
The steps were steep, the steps were wet,
Stopping halfway up to dry the sweat.

The break was good, we caught our breath,
Just long enough to start afresh.
Then up and up we didn't stop,
Until we reached the gate at top.

A single track of mud and grime,
At the quarry fence, we turned to climb.
Now blackened soil is all around,
But patches of heather reclaim the ground.

A foothold here and a foothold there,
All peppered with droppings from the Mourne hare.
With pains in neck and hands on knees,
We took a break to face the breeze.

Then looking back from where we'd come,
To Dundrum Bay in the morning sun.
I turned around to face the hill,
With aching limbs, I summoned the will.

Up and up and up we went,
No more I thought, my energy's spent.
I gave and gave, and the mountain took,
I lifted my head for one last look.

A cairn of stones came into view,
The summit! I cried with strength anew.
The final push, the final gasp.
The adrenalin rush, the top at last.

1911 CENSUS

Elizabeth McCann

His clever fingers
tapped the keys,
and tapped,
and tapped.
Information flared,
and changed,
and then
in black
pulling my eyes,
there it was,
My Mother's Name
11 months.

Sudden pleasure

caught my throat.

And images

zig-zagged,

reeled,

unravelled,

kaleidoscoped,

from then to then.

And for a moment

She was in my eyes, my ears.

More clicks

and we travelled back,

to names that made us.

THE NEWCASTLE SNAKE

Harry Mitchell

She lies and welcomes all who come,
They travel from near and far.
They form a snake as they make their way here,
In each and every car.

The snake it slithers towards its prey,
Expelling gas and noise.
It wraps itself around her streets,
But she doesn't lose her poise.

The snake explodes into the wind,
Sending shards in each direction.
She depends on every one of us,
To offer her protection.

They marvel at her beauty,
From the mountains to the sea.
They breath the marvellous salty air,
That makes them feel so free.

They gorge on fast food they have bought,

Their wrappers discarded, no bins have they sought.

They've tarnished the beauty of this wonderful town,

It should have been left as it was found.

It's time for the snake to now reform,

And slither back to where it was born.

Poor town! She lies and weeps,

Through Shimna and Glen, until the time of 5am.

When Council workers don their gear,

They've streets to clean and waste to clear.

They restore her to her natural beauty,

She's proud to perform her lifelong duty.

She lies and welcomes all who come,

They travel from near and far.

FATHER'S DAY

Siobhan McElroy

We have a love and hate relationship you see,
We never did see eye to eye, Him and Me!
Brought up in an unconventional family,
has left its scars deep inside of me.
Love and Confusion, Love and Confusion!

There was music all the time. Lots of friends
and flowing wine, experimenting, getting high
just to see the blue sky! Making sense of it all,
had to leave, before I hit the wall!
Love and Confusion, Love and Confusion.

He came to visit me last week,
A lot of words but didn't speak!
Hugs and kisses all around,
Now that I'm a chef in London Town!

We have a love and hate relationship you see.

We never did see eye to eye, Him and Me,

I'm beginning now to see the Old Man is a lot like Me.

Understanding Him is understanding We!

No more Confusion, No more Confusion,

No more confusion, only Love.

FOGGY WINDOWS

Lee Harding

They say the trip is worthwhile, that once the crying and biting in the backseat calms, that everyone will settle to enjoy the view. Donard and Commodagh will cast a gentle shadow over Newcastle's shores and once set free, my girls will run along the promenade while my wife and I stroll together, hand in hand.

Not today.

Today, the rain clouds greet us with a clammy hand that wraps around our throats and squeezes until our lungs begin to fail. That bubbling in the pit of our stomachs that churns into our throats as the heating blasts from the vents. The queues plod two car forwards and one van back, glum expressions mirroring the grey skies.

Once parked, I contemplate the next four hours of trudging through the crowds with the stench of plastic raincoats pressed against my nostrils. My wife screaming at me to watch the kids as they race to the amusements and my wallet depleting as eager little hands stretch out for more, more, more!

As she tries in vain to round the troops and dress them for battle, I elbow away the condensation, hoping against hope to see a jutting peak or forest trail. Yet, all is grained and awash with regret of what could have been.

She kicks me in the side as she twists and turns with no apology forthcoming. We are beyond that now, she doesn't say; a silent reminder of how times have changed between us.

The umbrella is in the boot: Dad's domain. My hand rests on the handle but I pause. I stare through the streaked mist into a world of promised adventure and my shoulders drop. Surely there is more than this?

I think to my own father and countless others who had to slide on that same solemn face. This sodden reality has washed away our dreams of pioneering conquests. The family ideal seemed to sparkle once upon a time like a diamond set in a band of polished gold. Now, its lack of lustre is as dimmed as these foggy windows and our lot in life is to try and beat back the black clouds and our hopes beneath a barrier of submission.

As I pull the handle the squabbling stops and the air hums still. I turn to find myself alone, not even the ghosts to keep me company. Their high-pitched shrills echo through my ears but their source is long since gone. I rub the point of my elbow but the bruising has snaked around my body to scar the empty chamber of my heart.

Take all the beauty, sunny days, and lofty peaks and cast them in the sea. Please, I beg, return me to those foggy windows.

MOON BEAM ROOM

Peter McCarron

Sleep walks on moonbeam road
Crossing points in time and place,
Meeting familiar memory friends
Shared life's journey with good grace.

Souls in human form meet
In unexpected ways,
Attraction spark ignites
Inner searching plays.

What are the possibilities
To develop a friendship,
Positives outweigh the negatives.
Compatible in relationship.

Shared stories relevant
A life journey begun,
Bond in hearts and minds
And may we become one.

When love flows

The heart glows

And excitement grows.

AUTUMN

RATHFRILAND RED KITES

Liz Laird

Three kites, sky cycling, screech, and whistle chimes.

The wind roars out in swirling ancient rhyme.

And I, a gardener, starting new enthralled,

soar heavenwards in tune, from fertile soil.

The River Bann is also fledgling here, trickling silver,

but today, is gushing froth in torrent fever.

A November morning after heavy rain,

finds me savouring freedom in Rathfriland terrain.

PLOUGHING FIELDS

Peter McCarron

A large beech tree, partially hidden by an overgrown hawthorn hedge, provided the perfect viewing platform for a shy, local boy. Brian, at twelve years old, spent many happy days perched in that tree after school. He patiently watched Shire Horses, "Ben" and "Tom," plough a field below the Mourne Mountains.

Day by day the Shires ploughed closer to Brian's position. The tree was conveniently situated near to the end point of each furrow. Each afternoon, at roughly the same time, Hughie, the ploughman, brought the horses to a halt. They completed another furrow, exposing the dark brown, rich soil. He used his powerful voice and tongue-clicks to command the horses. The long reins were loosely tied off at the plough. Hughie walked a short distance, filled two large buckets of fresh water from a drinking trough, and placed them in front of the horses. The buckets were refilled until they had enough. Ben and Tom lifted their heads and watched Hughie return with feeding nose-bags. They uttered their guttural approval and began eating their meals.

On the firm grass banking, beside the trough, Hughie ate sandwiches and drank from his flask. Familiar thoughts reappeared in his consciousness. 'One day, I will plough fields with my own horses, instead of following my retired Father's strict orders.'

As the work continued, Hughie knew he was being observed from the beech tree. On the last pass, he waved and shouted to the boy to join him. On the ground, Brian approached shyly. Unhooked from the plough, Tom and Ben were free to go to the trough beside the bolted gate.
"What's your name" Hughie asked.
"Brian"
"Do you live around here?"
"I live just across that field," Brian replied, pointing to the road.
"Would you like to sit on Tom's back?"
Brian nodded excitedly. The horses moved together with Hughie on Ben's back.

The road came too soon for Brian, who dismounted with Hughie's help. Brian watched Hughie and the horses disappear from view. Gleefully, Brian returned home to tell his younger brother and older sister about his adventures.

SHADOWLAND

Liz Laird

You basked in the exquisite pretence that all was swell.
Fantasy and reality boiled together in hard sell.
The lure that took you to live in Shadowland,
where like a child, you took to building castles in the sand.

In Shadowland, you walked the pathway towards invisibility.
The welcomes you provided painted me in shades of hypocrisy.
The Midnight Blue told you what you already knew.
Under cover of darkness, there becomes less and less of you.

In a reality check, it just took two sideway steps to regain the light.
And in so doing, I generated a shadow insight.
This reckoning gave me a time to pause,
recast the Future, and from the Past, withdraw.

AN UNCERTAIN WELCOME

Liz Laird

Uncertainty has at last caught up with me.
The opening of heart was the key that unlocked
an armoured mindset, and taught body melee.
Possibilities flood in, and do out-fox
man-made dams, generating a welcome release,
from the rush, rush, of an over-managed peace.

A shadowland lure unexpectedly set me free, to leap
through old chains visible, and invisible.
The direction's clear from Dundrum's Castle Keep
in sun-glinted waterways from Keel Point to Kilkeel.
Along the abandoned railway, the curlews wade
where once trains powered in, on the make, and trade.

To the south, a bastion of sentries makes a stand.
Donard, Commedagh and Bearnagh, granite built.
Firmly, they hold time still, and our storms withstand,
enabling us to find ourselves, and perspectives tilt.
I am not free, if control I do not bend.
Uncertainty, I am ready now, to be your friend.

NIGHT DUTY

Siobhan McElroy

"God Bless King Billy, God Bless the Pope."
Hospital ward, Mantra of his Hope!
Thought in my head, smile on my face,
Covering his bases, at the end of his race.
Did anyone listen? Did anyone care?
Wisdom of years lost in the air.
Prophet in our midst, could this be true?
God Bless King Billy, and the Pope too!

Holding his hand, his voice growing dim,
Our spirits, together, in comforting him.
His final prayer, his plea to us
"Only in God, Must We Trust".
Prophet in our midst, was this True?
God Bless King Billy, the Pope,
And all of Us too!

IN DONARD FOREST

Elizabeth McCann

The rain fell hard all night

Now

The water not gently slipping over the stones

Has swollen

And billows out

In lacy sheets

The music makes me stop and listen

MISSING YOU IS MY MOURNE MOUNTAIN VIEW

Siobhan McElroy

The sky is grey and the mountains are blue,
Sun is trying to peep through!
And all I can think about
is missing you, Missing You!

Your sweet smile, and your quirky way
see me through every day,
Now that you're gone
the sky is grey, mountains are blue,
Sun is trying to peep through!

You call me every night at nine
to let me know that you are mine,
Soon you'll be coming back to me
and all our senses will be free!

The sky won't be grey, the mountains won't be blue,

the sun, it will be shining through!

And all I can think about

is holding you,

Holding you!

A do be, do be, do be,

Do!

THE NEWCASTLE HARBOUR SWIMMERS

Harry Mitchell

To those who don't know, come rain hail or snow,
A rare group of swimmers, some seasoned, some beginners,
Arrive each morning at the Newcastle slip,
With a burning desire to go for a dip.

Wet suits are banned or so I'm told,
Hats, gloves and socks should keep out the cold.
To some the swell is a bit of a warning,
But fear is dispelled with shouts of "Good Morning".

Girls change on the slip, men on the rocks,
With shoes upturned to keep dry the socks.
There's a bit of a nip as bare feet hit the slip,
Then it's strip with haste and get into the waist.

Now this is the time you begin to wonder,
How cold will it be when you get down under?
A lunge, a plunge and off you go,
With squeals not of fright, but of sheer delight.

The time has come to head for the Buoy,
If you don't make it, it's enough to annoy.
To the Buoy, to the Buoy, to the Buoy they strive,
And a sense of relief as they all arrive.

Now to some this distance will be enough,
Especially if the sea's quite rough.
To others the second Buoy is a must,
In this, strong swimmers must put their trust.

Once there take time to look from the sea,
Sure, there's nowhere else you'd rather be.
The time has come to head for home,
Before the chill gets to the bone.

Now home, changing rooms would be nice,
For soon the rain will turn to ice.
A rub down and warm clothes is all it takes,
Just add a hot drink to stop the shakes.

Now starts the familiar dance of the sea,
This looks like someone needing a pee.
A chat, a laugh, no time for sorrow,
Sure, they'll all be back same time tomorrow.

THE WATERFALL

Lee Harding

The old man stood by the entrance to the waterfall with his fist pressed against his heart.

The cascading roar drowned away his dripping tears as he peered into the darkness. He had straightened to the point of pain, his wheezing chest quivering, his cane pushed firm within the mire to keep him steady as his gaze refused to move. He tilted his head as if hearing a distant echo but his stare never left the hollow crack where only a stooped and humble soul could crouch and enter.

"Good afternoon."

The abrupt welcome caused the old man to snap away but only for a moment. He barely registered the young hiker walking up the trail and swung his head back to its sole intent.

The hiker gazed at the elderly gentleman standing at the mouth of the falls wearing nothing but his nightgown. It flapped in the strong breeze that whipped down from the drumlins. There was no backpack, no sign of water, no morsel of food. The old man's knees were caked in muck and the hiker noticed a pair of handprints on the ground.

"Sir, are you feeling well today?"

The old man's mouth opened a fraction but no words slipped

out. Instead, his tears flowed in incessant rivulets, mirroring the contours of the rocks and the water gushing past.

The young hiker looked around for signs of support. Surely the old man had not travelled alone? The way was steep, the gravel too sharp for slippers, and the onset of autumn had floored a slippery challenge for the most arduous of cragsmen. There was no mode of transport. Indeed, the trail bore the tell-tale clues of a shuffle and stick that ended where the old man now stood.

"I want to know if I can help."

The old man sensed the stranger once more. The hiker's shadow had breached his line of sight to the mouth of the cave and so, with no other option, he turned to face him.

The young hiker had wondered at the water on the old man's face. He had hoped it was the splash of the river but saw the sad truth in the brimming eyes.

"Tell me what has happened."

The old man's fist remained steadfast. It thrust against his chest as if holding his soul within its cage and one false move would release it. Even through the cacophony, the hiker could hear a soft cry flow from the wizened lips:

"It's my time."

The old man cast his gaze through the waterfall and the young hiker followed in his wake. What force had driven against the elements and nature itself to make this man stand before the void in nothing but his nightwear?

The old man stepped forwards. The trail ended at the foot of the falls, the water crashing on the granite floor many feet below. His sodden slipper barely clung onto the fallen leaves. They formed a garish tapestry of dirty browns and gangrene yellows knitted together by slippery slime. He would surely tumble with one false move. Or one deliberate stride.

"Please, sir. Step back from the edge. It's not safe."

Rather than heed the warning, it spurred the old man on. He dragged his cane towards the precipice but it caught between two rocks. The spell broke and he blinked, looking around as if he knew neither where he was nor why his body had not obeyed.

"Where's my Daisy?"

The young hiker acted upon the confusion. He grasped the old man's hand and cupped it like he would a butterfly. Two drooping eyelids mirrored his own as the men stood opposite each other within the shadow of the Mournes.

"Everything is going to be okay."

Etched amongst the wrinkles of time was a palpable sadness. It formed from the old man's forehead and seeped down his pores to his nose and frowning face. Spittle foamed at the corners of his mouth like the froth from the lip of the falls.

"Is Daisy your wife?"

A simple nod confirmed the story that had conjured in the hiker's mind. He searched again for signs of assistance but the pair remained alone along the trail.

"Please. Tell me about her."

An infinitesimal light sparked within the old man's pupils. His weeping ceased and a slight smile broke through the haze.

"This is where we first kissed," he said. "It was autumn. We walked together up the hill. I was sure of my love but Daisy never shared in that way. I had to be certain. I would either walk down a happy man or..." His voice trailed as he comprehended the darkness. "A broken soul."

The young hiker squeezed the old man's fingers. The distraction brought him back to the present.

"Did you marry her?"

The old man nodded with a brighter decorum. "Her hair shone like the sun as we danced until dusk. Then we laughed and loved until the break of dawn. Ever since our first kiss, I vowed to never leave her. And I never have."

The hiker's thumb rubbed against the old man's wedding ring. The polished gold pressed into the sagging flesh, too embedded to ever be removed. There was one more question he had to ask.

"What would Daisy want you to do?"

Confusion spilt over the old man as if the hiker had poured water over his head. He pulled away, releasing the younger man's grip to fall by his waist. Seeing the reaction, the hiker pushed his palms together in prayer.

"You fought to be here, this special spot that means so much. I am a stranger and you are my elder, but I know that your love for her will never die. Don't let it end you."

He bowed and backed away. The old man watched him leave, tagging the trail that he and his wife had followed many decades before until vanishing below the horizon. The stiff breeze returned and his legs shuddered at the intrusion. He gripped his stick and faced the void once more. Within the darkness was where he longed to be. Only on the other side could they be united. It was his time.

His will forced his foot forwards but something deeper kept it still. He tried again, using the cane for leverage yet an unseen force forced it back. The echo of the young hiker's words resounded through the clatter of the falls and pierced his soul. This very spot had birthed true love, sealed by a kiss. That promise had never died even if he longed for existence to end. And that was something his Daisy would never want.

Broken, he fell to his knees. His shoulders heaved as the grief flooded out. He wanted to be with her but his time had not yet come. Breaching the waterfall was a journey, not his to pursue. She would be waiting on the other side when his journey finally ended. Until then, he would endure.

A warm set of arms embraced him from above. He looked up to see the young hiker wrap a coat around him. They struggled as one to bring him to his feet and then together they set off down the hill.

WINTER

NEWCASTLE FISHING DISASTER

Harry Mitchell

On the morning of Friday the 13th of January 1843, a number of men and boys in their skiffs were carried across Dundrum Bay by a favourable southerly wind, to the fishing grounds some eight miles off the Mourne coast, County Down. They were engaged in their occupation of line fishing for a short while, when a tremendous squall sprung up from the north-west the crews were unable to contend with the fierce wind, waves, cold and snow and most perished trying to reach shore.

Now follows a poem of that fateful day.

The Aftermath

On bended knee the townsfolk prayed,
The gossip passed, "They must be dead".
The storm has lasted far too long,
A young girl sang a mournful song.

With saddened hearts they drifted away,
As a peaceful calm reclaimed the bay.
"Look a man!" a woman was screaming,
Twas then they thought she must be dreaming.

"Look there's another and there's some more,
As poor souls dragged themselves to shore.
The sea had returned some of its prey,
For 73 others they had to stay.

The tales were told of Demons wild,
Some even called it the Devil's Child.
Their boats were only made of wood,
Against such fury they were no good.

Many survivors were cold and broken,
Of that day some have never spoken.
Others re-told the horrors for years,
Those that listened were brought to tears.

The day had started off so well,
Before the ringing of Death's Bell.

"16 Fishing Skiffs set out from Dundrum Bay,
To make their living, it was their way.
The sea was calm the wind was fair,
The Demons slept quietly in their lair."

"The catch was good, they all could tell,

It was then they noticed how big the swell.

The cry went up "Let's turn for shore",

In horror they looked land was no more.

The cold wind strengthened bringing with it snow,

The fragile boats were hurled to and fro.

In older Skiffs some parts were rotten,

These were the first ones to the Bottom.

Others were chilled to the bone,

As their boats leap like salmon returning home.

All who survived the storm that day,

Were tormented by nightmares till they met the clay.

Now times were hard with little pay,

But money was collected most every day.

A penny here and Tuppens there,

Even the local gentry showed they could care.

Soon the collection began to grow,

This charitable donation built the Widows Row.

A row of cottages for the most destitute,

Out of such sadness came some good.

LAKESIDE VIEW
(CASTLEWELLAN FOREST PARK)

Peter McCarron

Traffic noise beyond lake shores
Competes with lapping waves.
In November's daylight, Sun
Warms me, through fading rays.

My heart feels Nature's Bounty.
Birds in bushes flap for space.
My peace with beauty shimmers,
Over this gentle place.

A sniffing dog checks my scent
His owner walks on by,
Unaware of my great peace,
Head turned for glancing eye.

Winter's cold competes with Sun,
To keep my attention.
Sun's reflective path, finding
West shore's pieces of lake's edge.

A great blessing upon me,
Having the time and space,
To enjoy and become one,
With this Castlewellan place.

Peace and tranquillity reaches
Deeply, into my Soul.
Meditation calms my being.
These moments make me whole.

SPIRIT OF WIND AND RAIN

Siobhan McElroy

Slieve Donard, Mount Rushmore,
Sea and Ocean apart
Neolithic Age,
Connected by your beating heart.
Saw the wound in your side
Rusty bucket left behind.
Nature with its healing hand
Filled the void with frozen rain,
Stood beneath icicles of light
Paid homage to this mystical sight.
Ballynoe Stone Circle attuned to you
Equinox summer and winter too!

Mount Rushmore, Slieve Donard,
Ocean and sea apart
Neolithic age,
Connected by your beating heart.
Oppressors violated your sacred site
Washington, Jefferson, Roosevelt, Lincoln,
Drained your veins of black.
Now in barrels stack!

Gold and Silver in their vaults

In God We Trust debris of human rust!

Black Elk's vision

The Six Great Grandfathers Plea

"West, East, North, South, Above and Below,

Kindness and Love",

His wisdom they failed to See.

Gael and Sioux, Choctaw too,

Slieve Donard, Mount Rushmore,

Spirit of Wind and Rain,

Your Healing Soul will one day soar again!

THE MARK

Lee Harding

I sat in the shadows to see who had been let out for the night.

Gerry was perched by the bar swirling the dregs of his whisky in an endless circle. Next to him, sat Sean, his chin propping up his head as he watched McDonnell clean the shot glasses. The bar tender himself held that glum expression of a man caught in the drudgery of a meaningless vocation.

Joe and Lenny bickered by the light of the fire as usual. Tonight's row centred on Saturday's scores. Fingers wagged while the flushness of their cheeks flamed to boiling point. Old Pat rose from his spot by the hearth but his pleas for calm only bolstered their spirits. With curses bouncing off the low ceiling, he threw his hands in the air and returned to study his prized pocket watch.

A roar rang from the McBride brothers who were joined by a group of folks I did not recognise. The strangers were indeed, if strange was an apt term, stranger still. One wore a billowed turban hat quite unlike the tartan cap pulled tight around my scalp. His clothes mimicked that of a cherry tree in full blossom. His pointed boots were lifted from the pages of an Arabian tale. His skin was darker than the sullen window shades yet the gleam of his smile suffused the sombre air.

The others were a mixed bag of shapes and sizes never seen in McDonnell's Cellar. A muscled man too wide to fit through the door beat his barrelled chest with two meaty paws. A young boy copied him but I noticed that his head was too large to belong to a child. I squinted through the darkness to uncover the oddity only heard in folklore. The leprechaun leapt onto the table and with his little legs a-jig, danced *The Wild Rover* while the McBrides sang along.

"Bloody carnies."

Dermot grumbled into his beard and drowned his sorrows in his pint. I leant over to ask him what he meant. He wiped the froth from his lips and pointed to the poster on the door.

"Circus is in town," he said as I gazed at the roaring lions and striped two-ring tent. "Don't trust any of them. Steal the eye out the back of your skull and take your purse behind your back."

"How come the McBrides have taken their fancy?" I asked, glancing at the brothers.

Dermot shrugged and returned to his drink leaving me in a state of confusion. Those lads seldom spent a penny on anyone but themselves. The leprechaun finished with a flurry, stamping his foot onto the table top and pushing his arms out wide. The McBrides took to their feet and ushered a wild applause just as the door barged inwards and two newcomers staggered in.

"Is anyone a doctor?"

The plea came from the hiker. I didn't recall his face but that's not unusual for these parts. The tavern sits beneath the foot of the Mournes and attracts those foolish enough to brave the winds of winter. He seemed to be made of sterner stuff with a neck you could hang meat on. I've met his type before, more of a local than many of the locals.

All stares were drawn to the man gripping his arm. He wore no pack, his shoes held no grip, and a gust of wind would have ripped his thin coat in half. He clutched at his chest as the hiker found an empty chair by the fire and lowered him down. McDonnell swung the bar top high and hurried to join them.

"What's wrong with him?"

"He's badly hurt. Something attacked him."

Did my ears deceive me? Something and not someone? The victim gave a moan that chilled the air to ice. The leprechaun was helped to the ground as the McBrides and the rest of the bar's motley crew drew closer.

"I found him on the path." The hiker thumbed over his shoulder towards the Granite Trail. Some of these men worked in the quarry before it closed last summer. "He was holding his stomach and kept repeating the same words over and over."

The hiker brought his fingers into the light of the fire. Even in the orange hue, I was drawn to the crimson stain. As if on cue, the victim cried out:

"The mark, the mark, it gave me the mark."

A gasp rang through the throng. We had all heard the legends since we were lads running through the forest. Our mothers warned us of what lay within the mountain's fringe. Those were yarns spun to keep us out of mischief. Sure, we used them with our own laddies and lasses. The blood seeping through the man's vest told a darker tale as he slumped in agony.

"I called for help," the hiker continued, "but none came. Holding my lamp with one hand, I managed to help him to his feet. We shuffled down the path towards the harbour. After each step, he tried to run but I held him fast for fear of falling. And all the while he cried, 'The mark. The mark'."

McDonnell turned to the rest of us with his brow furrowed. I had remained rooted on my seat. It offered the perfect vantage point. Or perhaps I was too afraid to move. Old Pat pointed to the long rips in the victim's shirt.

"Look, an animal has got him."

Gerry bent to inspect the ripped threads and nodded.

"Did you see anything on the trail?"

The hiker's body trembled. I was unsure whether it was fright or if he was freezing. As if reading my mind, one of the carnival folk shouted, "Get this man a drink."

McDonnell was torn between giving a free ale and saving a stranger's life. His conscious won out and he rushed to the bar.

"Here, drink this."

The hiker took the offering and tipped it down his throat. We held our breath as he continued his story.

"I made it to Donard's summit by noon. A fog descended so thick that it caught in my lungs. I held onto the wall, measuring each step of my descent, when a sound rang out from the haze. I have heard the cry of wolves before but this was a blood-curdling howl no animal could muster. My heart pounded within me as if my body knew that Death itself had arrived."

His hand shook as he returned the tankard. McDonnell refused to take it like it was cursed. The hiker dropped his chin to the floor.

"Something felt foul as if the fog had shot from the snout of the beast. I peered into the cloud trying to catch a glimpse but it kept just out of site as if toying with me. Even through the gales, I sensed it bearing its fangs. I groped around for a rock and cast it with all of might but it sailed past the creature. Or, perhaps, straight through it."

Sean towered above the men with his arms folded tight. Not one for tall tales, he smacked his lips together.

"A ghost, you say? Now, I've heard it all."

Old Pat pointed to the blood pooling on the floor. "Then what do you call this?" he cried. Joe and Lenny agreed. The circus strong man flexed his shoulders and slapped Old Pat on the back in solidarity. The McBrides nodded to each other while the hiker raised his neck to look at his detractor.

"When I regained my courage I made haste down the Dark Steps towards the quarry. The fog descended with me like a thick blanket wrapped around my throat. All the while, I knew the creature was following me. I could smell the stench of rotting meat. It might have been hidden within the mist but I swear to all the saints that it was as real as you or me."

Sean's distrust melted like wax as he saw the dread on the hiker's face. The strong man gripped onto his collar as if consoling the young man's worst fears. A high-pitched voice rose from beneath them.

"What is the mark?" the leprechaun said with a squeak.

At the mention of the word, the injured man threw back his head and let out a curdling wail. Gerry was so taken aback that he fell into the arms of the turban wearer who helped push him back onto his feet. The Arabian took off his hat to deliver the terrible answer.

"Although I am not from these parts my grandfather once passed through here. He told me of the attacks back in '23. Did you hear of them?"

The crowd shook their heads as did I.

"Two farmhands didn't come back from their trek to Binnion. They were gathering in the sheep for winter. After two days without word, the locals set out to find them. Their bodies were found hanging from an old oak tree. Their guts had gushed to the ground and a mark was cut into their chests."

"What did it look like?" Gerry stammered.

The injured man raised his arm and ushered Sean to help him up. With an agonising grimace, he ripped open his blood-soaked shirt. An intake of breath from all who beheld the sight silenced the bar. My vantage point was obscured by the strong man so I stood to my full height to see. There, carved into the poor soul's flesh, were five ragged claw marks.

"I fought it," the victim cried. "It leapt from the shadows and brought me down. I could feel it panting by my face as it snapped to bite it off. It tossed me from side to side, snapping my ribs. As my bones broke, I grabbed for my stick. It flipped me onto my back for the mortal blow when I struck out as hard as I could. Its haunting howls turned to agony as the wood pierced its hide. With one final swipe, it left its mark and fled back into the darkness."

Exhausted, the man collapsed into the chair. The leprechaun pushed through to press his fingers to his neck. He turned to McDonnell and said, "Pour him a whiskey."

The bar man obeyed. The leprechaun added: "Don't be so selfish. Can't you see we all need a drink?"

The McBrides helped to bring the drinks to the group. They downed the shots in one and crossed their hearts. The victim and hiker nodded their thanks while the turban wearer took control.

"We have medicine back in the caravans. If we leave now, we can stop the bleeding before he faints."

The strong man helped both men with ease. Soon, the carnival folk had rounded by the exit. They thanked everyone for their hospitality and asked for our prayers as they tended to the injured. Once the door shut, we stood in stunned silence.

"It can't be real," Sean said but his head and his heart did not agree. I myself was in shock at the markings on the poor man's chest. Somewhere within the Mournes a beast was lurking, ready to pounce on the next soul who ventured up there alone.

"You're all a bunch of fools."

Everyone turned to the only man still sipping his pint. Archie grumbled something and only spoke up when I asked him to.

"The only marks in here are you."

"What do you mean?"

"When you go to a circus they see you coming. They can spot a fool a mile away. The first one puts a mark on your back so the others know you're easy to part from your money."

I looked at the others and noticed something on old Pat's coat. It looked like a chalk line that ran from his shoulder to his waist. Pat pointed to Gerry who had the same mark too. As did Sean, Joe, Lenny, and the McBrides.

"They drank your drink for free, McDonnell. All to hear a tall tale from two strangers. And I'll wager that's not all they took."

The McBride brothers slapped their pockets looking for their money pouches. The others did likewise. All were empty and old Pat's pocket watch was missing too. They ran to the door and flung it open but the horses and cart were long gone.

"There's no point chasing them," Archie added with a laugh. "The circus finished tonight. You'd have more luck finding a monster in the Mournes."

HARBOUR LIGHTS

Liz Laird

Across the bay, Down Cathedral Angels
raise Christmas bells-a-clatter.
Brimmed to rafters, young and old
in carols, verse, and chatter.

The Harbour Lights peered warily,
through rain sheets a-clip-clopping-down,
as misty-eyed and memory-wrapped,
she drove the shore, homeward bound.

Old coastguard cottage kept watch,
whilst inside, the nestling lamp
and lazily the fireside warmth
cosied her, shedding the damp.

The rain ceased as her hand reached sleep.
A breeze was rapping a merry tune,
and gently danced white lace in sails
as her eyes shut soft on the moon.

At midnight, Donard and Commedagh
went striding the cloaked-damp-wind-wilds.
With Devil's Coach Road lurking close by
she dreamt dark safety, personified.

Towards dawn, the wind laid off its keening,
and within their sanctuary walls
the hobby boats bobbed playfully,
knowing she'll wake to the seagull's call.

Patterns in life, lulled by the tides,
washing over and under the sand.
Pillow-frothed truths cantering in.
Light on dark waters, mirroring soul of man.

A SNOWY NIGHT IN MOURNE

Harry Mitchell

The night was dark, the night was still,
you couldn't hear a sound.
Then one by one, flakes drifted down,
And settled, on our town.

The whitest blanket, delivered with care,
The purest fleece, would not compare.
And smothered, all sharp edges seen,
With flowing drifts, of white not green.

Then all at once a fox appears,
With auburn brush, and pointed ears.
His prints disturb the blanket new,
This only enhances the watcher's view.

They follow his meandering trail,
The mark of his feet, the drag of his tail.
His quest they know, is to find some food,
But with snow covered land, it is no good.

And then he wanders out of view,

No doubt in search of pastures new.

Steadily again, the snow doth fall,

Hiding that he was here at all.

COLD WINTER'S VIEW

Peter McCarron

White winter's remnants lay
Hoping longer to stay
For fellow flakes arrival
Challenging nature's survival.

Cold clouds of grey
Covering birds of prey.
Out of uncertain mist
A fox cub takes a risk.

A walk sniffed in stealth mode
Hoping for food on the road.
Joining mama fox and brother
Each red minding the other.

Sudden sounds interrupt
Three pairs of ears prick up.
Flashing lorry moves the snow
Road surface now on show.

Time to leave Mournes' high road

Find food and safe abode.

Searching and searching each day.

But night produces more prey.

A WINTER'S WALK UP DONARD

Harry Mitchell

A bitter cold crispness fills the morning air,
Woollen hats pulled tightly and down over hair.
Gnarled knuckled branches hang overhead,
As on a frozen carpet, of dead leaves we tread.

Red berries bursting, on the holly bush,
A ready-made breakfast, for the hungry thrush.
The gunshot snap, of a frozen root,
The ice breaking crunch, of the hiker's boot.

Steaming breaths searching, for the way to go,
Hesitant looks at a sky, heavy laden with snow.
Onward we march and up, the gradient increases,
Mouths gasp for air, as winded breath releases.

Scarfs and gloves, are now removed at will,
A welcome relief, to the winters chill.
All at once, snow covers the frozen ground,
Decision quickly made, let's turn around.

Boots skidding on hardened ground, with haste of descent.

Muscles aching all around, all our energy spent.

Home now, a nice warm drink, in front of open fire,

Contented feelings all around, of this I'll never tire.

DUNDRUM SPEAKEASY

Elizabeth McCann

The lights are dimmed
The singer sings
And misery drips
And we are there
Our little group
Bound together with scars of pain
Pass the tea and sympathy
Or the razor blades

But
The party is not over
As the singer says
And the sun will rise tomorrow
And we will count in days
And take pleasure in small things
So pass the tea and sympathy
Hold the razor blades

BIOGRAPHIES

Lee Harding is a writer of dark thrillers and psychological horrors. Living within the shadows of the Mournes, he has penned eight full-length novels and is an award-winning author. Visit www.leeharding.online to read his twisted tales.

Liz Laird is an artist and writer who lives in the foothills of the Mournes. She has enjoyed writing poetry since her teenage years, and more recently prose. She contributed to the development, writing and performance of 'First Responders' in the Playhouse Theatre, Derry, in years 2019 and 2020.

Elizabeth McCann was born in County Armagh. She lives in Newcastle, safely harboured between the mountains and the sea. Since a child, she has been a storyteller, scribbler, and play actor.

Peter McCarron lives in Newcastle with views of the Slieve Donard range. He writes poetry and short stories, humorous and serious. He was influenced by his Mother as "a word-smith" in the Irish oral tradition and his English teacher Seamus Deane.

Siobhan McElroy is a poet songwriter originally from Omagh, County Tyrone, now living in Downpatrick. Her inspiration comes from life experiences. Her poems have been read on BBC Radio Ulster Sunday with Brian D'Arcy.

Harry Mitchell rekindled his love of writing when he retired to Newcastle in 2017. His works include poetry, short stories and a comedy series written for local radio. Environmental awareness comes through passionately in a lot of Harry's writing.

Learn more about the Newcastle Writers' Group on our website:
www.newcastlewritersgroup.com

Printed by Amazon Italia Logistica S.r.l.
Torrazza Piemonte (TO), Italy